199 ideas

Building Meeting Attendance and Revenue

PUBLISHED BY
ASAE: THE CENTER FOR ASSOCIATION LEADERSHIP

WASHINGTON, DC

The contributors have worked diligently to ensure that all information in this book is accurate as of the time of publication and consistent with standards of good practice in the general management community. As research and practice advance, however, standards may change. For this reason it is recommended that readers evaluate the applicability of any recommendations in light of particular situations and changing standards.

ASAE: The Center for Association Leadership
Association Management Press
1575 I Street, NW
Washington, DC 20005-1103
Phone: (202) 626-2723; (888) 950-2723 outside the metropolitan Washington, DC area
Fax: (202) 220-6439
Email: books@asaecenter.org
We connect great ideas and great people to inspire leadership and achievement in the association community.

Keith C. Skillman, CAE, Vice President, Publications, ASAE: The Center for Association Leadership
Baron Williams, CAE, Director of Book Publishing, ASAE: The Center for Association Leadership
Cover design by Beth Lower, Art Director, ASAE: The Center for Association Leadership and Troy Scott Parker, Cimarron Design

This book is available at a special discount when ordered in bulk quantities. For information, contact the ASAE Member Service Center at (202) 371-0940.

A complete catalog of titles is available on the ASAE: The Center for Association Leadership website at www.asaecenter.org.

ISBN-13: 978-0-88034-328-2
ISBN-10: 0-88034-328-1

Printed in the United States of America.

CONTENTS

INTRODUCTION AND ACKNOWLEDGEMENTS

Revenue generated from meeting attendance registration, exhibit and trade show booth fees, and educational program fees represents a core element of most associations' nondues revenue sources. In fact, according to ASAE's *Operating Ratio Report, 13th Edition* (2008), they rank as the top three sources of nondues revenue for both trade and individual membership organizations. But is your organization maximizing the contribution those three sources of revenue are making to the bottom line? With the proportion of overall revenue that dues income accounts for trending downward, association and nonprofit leaders are always searching for additional nondues revenue. One way to accomplish that feat is to enhance the programs in place to get the most out of them.

This book contains 199 ideas that can help contribute directly or indirectly to the bottom line in the areas of attendance registration, exhibit/sponsor fees, and cost savings. Implementing just one idea has the potential to add dollars to your bottom line. Adopt or adapt the ideas that will work for your organization and use the others as a source of generating new ideas (see "Continue to Generate Creative Ideas on Your Own" contributed by Jeff Cufuade on pages 51 through 53). Or use these tips as a checklist to ensure you're doing everything possible to capitalize on all of your opportunities.

The tried-and-tested tactics in this latest addition to our ever-growing *199 Ideas* series were contributed from ASAE members and members of ASAE's Meetings and Exposition Council who have shared their knowledge so others may benefit. We hope you will consider giving back to the community by sharing a tip for possible inclusion in future publications. Check out the back pages of this book or go to **www.asaecenter.org/sharemytip**.

Our sincerest thanks goes to the following contributors and to all those who share their experiences through ASAE.

ASAE'S MEETINGS AND EXPOSITION COUNCIL CONTRIBUTORS

Hunter C. Clemens, CMP, Association Management Group

Mary Pat Cornett, CMP, CAE, American Academy of Otolaryngology—Head & Neck Surgery

Pamela S. Dallstream, CMP, CMM, Society of Critical Care Medicine

Pamela Dorsey, The Aluminum Association

Dawn M. Eagleton, Tourism Toronto

Carey Fenn-Moses, Salt Lake Convention & Visitors Bureau Eastern Region

Frank E. Gainer, American Occupational Therapy Association, Inc.

Jennifer Howie, Noble House Hotels & Resorts

Kerry Lambert, CMP, Arlington Convention & Visitors Bureau

Amy A. Ledoux, CMP, CAE, ASAE: The Center for Association Leadership

Laurie Meacham, The Broadmoor

Darren Mendola, CMP, Alzheimer's Association

Kimberly Miles, CMP, American Hotel & Lodging Association

Michele M. Miller, ConferenceDirect

Suzanne Payne, Ohio Dental Association

James A. Perrin, Starwood Hotels & Resorts

Michael E. Pramstaller, CAE, Print Services Distribution Association

Dominique M. Stumpf, CMP, National Pest Management Association

Clark Thomas, MPA, CAE, Association Innovations LLC

Heidi A. Voorhees, CAE, Institute of Food Technologists

Allison Wachter, CEM, ASAE: The Center for Association Leadership

OTHER CONTRIBUTORS

Karen S. Barnett, Professional Landcare Network
Melissa Bowers, ASAE: The Center for Association Leadership
Deb Brawner, CMP, ASAE: The Center for Association Leadership
Bill Burns, CAE, Association for Play Therapy
Linda S. Chreno, CAE, IOM, American College of Phlebology
Margaret Core, Biotechnology Industry Organization
Jeffrey Cufaude, Idea Architects
Diana Dabdub, American Society of Health-System Pharmacists
Tara Dunion, CEA and the International CES
Joan Eisenstodt, Eisenstodt Associates LLC
Dave Fellers, CAE, Dave Fellers Consulting, LLC (DFC)
Valerie Jane Fries-Wade, MA, International Right of Way Association
Peter Hutchins, American Forests
Jenna Kellam, Maryland Association for Justice, Inc.
Rozella Kennedy, American Indian Science and Engineering Society
Rich Lapin, TAPPI
Amy Castaldi Nostrand, CMP, Leadership Synergies
Scott D. Oser, Scott Oser Associates
John Parke, CMP, Leadership Synergies
Corrie Pelc, California Optometric Association
Kelly Price, CEM, ASAE: The Center for Association Leadership
Ann Ranson, CSR-3 Marketing
Jessica Tennant, ASAE: The Center for Association Leadership
Pamela Troop, CMP, ASAE: The Center for Association Leadership

ATTENDEE ENGAGEMENT AND SATISFACTION

1. Have a user of your product participate in a trade show booth as a testimonial and encourage buyer-to-buyer relationships.

A vendor invites a key customer to provide testimonials, which encourages prospective buyers who are unfamiliar with the products and services and creates an openness to discuss opinions with a peer.

2. Provide exclusive access as a reward to special constituencies in your membership.

If you've ever had the good fortune to be the holder of a backstage pass for a concert featuring one of your favorite performers, you know the spirit behind this idea. The possibilities are endless: special sessions or meal functions for individuals holding certifications, special events for young professionals, invitation-only access to small-group discussions with general session speakers or other high-profile individuals, or sneak previews of new association services being offered to early adopters or thought and opinion leaders among your members. Some organizations also use special access as a way to raise money for their PACs or foundation-related efforts.

3. Create a Flickr Photo Pool where anyone can add photos. People like seeing people.

Show the images in real time so people can see what else has been happening and see real photos of their friends learning, enjoying, and engaging at the conference.

4. Consider a fishbowl room configuration to enhance attendees' experience during learning sessions.

Consider everyone in the room to be on the panel as opposed to a few select individuals speaking from the stage. Set a room in a fishbowl or other modified theater-style setting to encourage intimacy and interaction among all participants and create the space for a powerful conversation of the whole. Start with a strong moderator/facilitator who feels confident working with the full group. A few lead panelists sit in the inner circle of the fishbowl or are scattered strategically among all the attendees. These individuals would come prepared to offer some provocative thoughts and to "seed" the conversation, but the session's emphasis would be on tapping into everyone's wisdom and insights. Have the moderator remind all participants to introduce themselves every time they address the full group. Experiment with other space and seating styles, like an open-space lounge, to enhance the learning experience.

5. Using trade publications as strategic partners can be beneficial.

Ask publishers from industry trade publications to host free educational seminars on the exhibit floor in theater areas. This provides exposure for the partner while generating additional programs which can improve the attendee's experience.

6. Create community by assisting attendees in social settings to easily connect with like-minded peers.

Divide your reception room by geographic region, content areas of interest, or common concerns. Locate your food and beverage in a centralized common area. Designate the individual areas with signage, pipe and drape, or in other ways that make it easy for people to find the spot and people they are seeking.

7. Increase attendee and buyer engagement.

Host receptions and/or breakfasts on the trade show floor for additional key buyer and supplier engagement outside of regular exhibiting hall hours.

8. Create attendee engagement by constructing a scavenger hunt game.

Break into groups and engage in a scavenger hunt in an opening session. The hunt can be for tangible or intangible items. Tangible items would include things they must find and either note where they are or actually bring back with them. Intangible items would include finding examples of leadership, innovation, creativity, teamwork, encouragement, or living the mission of the organization.

9. Set up several "Idea Exchange Centers" at strategic locations on the exhibit hall floor.

Throughout the conference, hold several sessions focusing on "hot topics." Each session would have a topic leader and would be held on the exhibit hall floor. These informal gatherings produce opportunities to network on specific topics with peers without leaving the show floor.

10. Prior to the conference, survey attendees to get their feedback about what they would like to see happen during the meeting.

Send a survey to past attendees and preregistered attendees to gather feedback about what session topics would most interest them, their expectations for the meeting, and other needs.

11. Foster buy-in with member content and experienced task forces.

Engage members in the creation of program content and member experience by recruiting past attendees and/or members. Members will appreciate that you solicited their opinion. This will help create relevant content and will develop buy-in and spokespeople for the meeting and the organization.

12. Create gathering places for attendee interaction.

Create comfortable gathering places throughout the meeting with lounge furniture. To save costs on furniture, use blow-up couches and chairs, creating colorful, inviting, and inexpensive areas for people to relax and connect. You can give the lounge areas fun names like "Hot Air Lounge."

13. Find ways to extend the onsite learning experience.

Work with your keynote presenters and/or their representing speakers' bureaus to provide the speakers' latest book to the audience as a gift and to extend the attendees' experience and tie it to the meeting long after the meeting is over.

14. Provide tours of the conference area.

Have trained staff or volunteers available to give tours of the conference area to first-timers and any other interested parties. These individuals should be well-versed in some of the commonly asked questions. As an alternative, create a PowerPoint presentation, a video or virtual tour (perhaps when on your site visit) that participants can view and/or download in advance. All these tools should guide participants through the various elements of your conference and their respective locations.

15. Build participation with Foursquare.

This geo-location resource is a Smartphone app that allows people to "check in" to different locations at your meeting. The GPS functionality of Foursquare allows users to see which of their friends are nearby and to identify other nearby check-in locations. It is a useful app for event organizers that serves to drive attendees to specific events, exhibits, sessions, and venues.

16. Utilize biographies to create connections amongst attendees and exhibitors.

Use online tools to populate information about the exhibiting companies as well as the exhibitors. This sharing of information will lead to a growing understanding of products and services offered in corporate social media links on each profile. Creating a profile of each attendee, including their photo, full contact details, and other information, can be very helpful to exhibitors. Compile the information into an online directory that can be shared with other attendees and exhibitors. (Allow participants to opt out as well.)

17. Create cross-functional teams for brainstorming ideas to enhance the onsite attendee experience.

Work with the internal membership, education, sponsorship, media, and other departments to create cross-functional teams for brainstorming conference ideas. Staff members from the other teams may provide valuable insights and new ideas for enhancing the attendee experience. Bringing staff together in this way can also help to avoid communication silos.

18. Encourage attendees in educational sessions to respond to the questions and challenges of other attendees.

Give each participant a mailing envelope and encourage them to write their questions or challenges on the outside. Envelopes are then posted on the wall and other participants are invited to offer responses on index cards, which are deposited in the envelopes. Tip: Post a few examples and solution cards so people get a better sense of how to contribute.

19. Create sponsorship offerings that incorporate elements of social responsibility that clearly reflect the organization's values.

In an effort to drive loyalty and partnership, create sponsorship opportunities that not only drive revenues, but also give back to the community. Sponsor committees should be formed to ensure their voices are heard in developing the process and in identifying opportunities that are meaningful to all.

20. Offer social responsibility team-building activities.
Present a team-building activity that focuses on corporate/social responsibility that also ties in to your organization's mission or the local community in which your meeting resides. Attendees would have an opportunity to network and exercise leadership skills while giving back to the organization and community.

21. Create a new member welcoming experience.
Enhance the experience of new members by providing mentoring and special networking opportunities, reserved seating, a networking lounge, orientation sessions, and a tour of the facility to help them navigate the meeting. Consider providing a sticker, ribbon, or pin to first-time attendees so staff, volunteers, and other attendees can easily identify new participants and help welcome and guide them.

22. Establish a welcoming committee to generate a sense of hospitality and appreciation for all who attend.
Solicit volunteers to serve as part of your meet-and-greet team. This team can welcome participants at particular events and make people feel that they're an important part of the organization. Orient the team so everyone is clear on the goals for the effort, including greeting people, thanking them for coming, and reaching out to individuals who look confused. Train them to be able to answer common questions about your meeting. Involve them at registration and at important places, such as outside general sessions, exhibit halls, and banquets.

23. Enhance first-timers' experiences with "First Friends."
Avoid socially uncomfortable moments by soliciting volunteers who agree to serve as "First Friends." One of the potentially intimidating moments for first-timers is the opening reception where old friends reunite and first-timers stand by themselves. During your first major social event, First Friends reach out to the first-timers, engage them in conversation, and introduce them to other individuals at the event. The goal of First Friends is to make the first-timers feel comfortable and part of the group without calling great attention to their newcomer status or to the hosting role that First Friends are playing.

24. Add fitness activities to your event to engage attendees and promote healthy lifestyles.

Identify association members and suppliers to lead fitness and exercise activities throughout the meeting. Offer fitness events, such as a Fun Run & Walk, early rise-and-shine yoga classes, and the like, prior to the start of educational sessions. The events can serve as networking opportunities and offer healthy activities for attendees. Ensure that interaction and a sense of community is built into activities. Help attendees honor their commitment to health and well-being!

25. Start several sessions with interaction and engagement.

Turn up the lights and encourage attendees to engage! Possibilities include displaying association trivia questions on the screen like movie theater trivia, using electronic polling and measuring attendees' perspectives on various issues, or having cards on seats that ask people to introduce themselves to those around them and answer a specific question about themselves or the meeting.

26. Work with sponsors to think outside the box when creating visibility opportunities.

Work with sponsors to help them identify unique sponsor offerings that will bring awareness to their organization/company while helping to deliver a better attendee experience. These opportunities could range from providing a themed break, a signature cocktail, a unique lounge, an entertainment activity, or an attendee gift that they can use at the meeting (like a reusable water bottle, tote bag, jump drive, and more).

27. Offer face-to-face meetings over online meetings whenever possible.

Providing attendees with an online option is great for meetings where attendees have to travel far, but if you are only pulling locally and the meeting is small to begin with, have everyone attend in person. In-person interactions are much more valuable.

28. Incorporate icebreakers into your meeting.

Break the monotony of conference orientations by including some simple introduction exercises during each orientation session.

Conference orientation can sometimes feel like parades of people each offering little snippets of information about the program. Instead of having all talking heads, engage community members in an interactive game that will help them learn about various conference components. Possibilities include creating a board game, playing a Jeopardy-style quiz game, having a matching exercise, and distributing slips of paper with either a question or an answer and having people find the question or answer that matches their paper. "Mass People Bingo" challenges participants to find people in the room who match descriptions like *someone who's been an association member for at least five years* or *someone who has served as an association volunteer.* Once the folks have introduced themselves, have them initial the square on their bingo card that matches their description. The person who fills the most squares in a certain amount of time (not just a "bingo") wins a prize.

29. Let your attendees choose which sessions will be presented at your meeting.

Crowd source some of your content leaders' session topics or themes for general sessions where attendees can suggest ideas and/or presenters, and others can vote on which they like best.

30. Use handheld technology devices to connect attendees with common interests and goals.

Use technology to connect attendees during the conference. Handheld devices such as "SpotMe" can be used to connect attendees onsite. The devices can alert an attendee when someone they would like to meet is nearby, or help people to electronically trade business cards. Solicit session evaluations and feedback through mobile device texting.

31. Use Twitter as a free audience response system to increase interaction.

Teach presenters to use Twitter hash tags to let attendees respond to questions in sessions via their Smartphones. Presenters can integrate feedback opportunities for interaction and assign a hash tag to each response. The presenter can track responses via their TweetDeck.

32. Employ mobile food carts to help increase exhibit hall traffic.

Put specialty food items on a mobile food cart. Move the cart around the floor to help increase traffic in low trafficked areas. Attendees can track the food cart through your conference Twitter account.

33. Help your attendees connect through a speed-meet activity.

Create a one- to two-hour time slot at your meeting where you have attendees sit across from each other for two minutes. Then rotate to be able to meet 50 to 100 new attendees before the meeting even starts.

34. Plan a "Tweet Up" to connect members who have interacted virtually via Twitter.

Set up times and places to gather your tweeps face-to-face throughout your event. The members who have communicated virtually will enjoy the in-person connection. Other members can come to learn how to use Twitter and join the virtual community. Offer ribbons or stickers to identify your tweeps throughout the show.

35. Create a "return on experience" packet for attendees that helps them maximize learning information gained onsite.

Develop a kit that helps attendees take the ideas and concepts learned at the meeting back to their organization to show the value of having attended.

36. Create and run a "Who is here?" slideshow.

Ask attendees to share two to three interesting things about themselves prior to the event and submit a picture. Create a slideshow and run it continuously during arrivals so attendees can learn more about each other.

37. Use team-building concepts to create excitement on the show floor and in general sessions.

Ask participants to wear specific colors, components, or industry logo-wear to show their pride. Create friendly competition (puzzles, trivia, game show format, etc., using industry or conference information) to build affinity among chapters, geographic locations, or sectors of the industry. Reward winners with fun prizes or convention rewards such as drink tickets, logo ware, organizational discounts, etc.

38. Create an exhibitor/sponsor concierge.

Have a dedicated staff person or volunteer whose role is to make certain that exhibitors and sponsors receive all benefits promised.

39. Provide an Exhibitor Resource/Supply area.

Create an area by the exhibitor show office or in the exhibit hall that provides common tools and supplies for exhibitors to utilize. This area can have building tools, scissors, tape, twine, boxes, note pads, pens, mints, band aids, hand sanitizer, water, and more. Your exhibitors will love you for it!

40. Create a Business Connection Lounge to let the buyer–seller engagement continue.

For organizations that have exhibit hall hours that do not go all day, consider creating a Business Connection Lounge for exhibitors to take their clients or meet as a team when the show floor is closed. This lounge can have a variety of work areas so exhibitors can meet as a staff team or to deliver a presentation to a customer or simply as a place just to relax and have a casual conversation with customers or colleagues when the show hours are over.

41. Include fun ribbons for attendees.

Provide ribbons that reflect qualities such as "motivator," "visionary," "party animal," etc., to allow attendees to reflect their personality. Also, use blank ribbons with an indelible marker to allow attendees to create their own customized ribbon.

42. Conduct surveys to improve customer satisfaction.

Conduct surveys with attendees, exhibitors, and staff to obtain direct feedback on processes and procedures. These surveys can be done with mobile kiosks at registration, via email, through a mobile application, through focus groups, in talk-back sessions, and even by secret shoppers at your meeting who observe and talk with attendees and exhibitors.

43. Let your exhibitors know you care by enlisting "Booth Thankers."

Enlist volunteers (Board members, other volunteer groups, and members) and even staff to visit exhibitors to thank them and get their direct feedback. Provide "booth thanker" packets to your volunteers with their list of booths to visit, a map of where those booths are located, and forms with a few key questions to ask exhibitors in order to solicit their feedback. Reward your booth thankers with an event ticket or even a discount for a future meeting.

44. Pre-populate the electronic registration form with information from the previous year.

Pre-populate online registration with information from the previous year's event. The registration will not be complete until the current payment information is added. Attendees will have the opportunity to change/confirm address and contact information.

45. Have meeting staff provide ROI reports or value statements to supporters.

An ROI value statement can be offered based on organization calculations and assessments prior to and during an event with a final report offered post-show. This allows the organization to help set the equations and measurements of ROI while also influencing supporters to utilize such metrics in the future.

46. Offer compelling conversations with key association leaders.

Schedule informal, brief conversations between members and association leaders. This allows leaders to present key information about the organization and the event in a casual setting, and provides an opportunity to collect feedback from attendees.

47. Go beyond the basic badges.

Give attendees the opportunity to include nontraditional information about themselves to enhance their networking experience. For example: Twitter handle, Facebook screen name, interests, expertise, hobbies, etc. The organization could provide stickers or symbols to allow people to communicate these activities visually on their badges. This will help attendees make connections, share information, and foster discussion. It also shows that you recognize members as individuals and are willing to "go the extra mile" to help them show their uniqueness.

48. Offer a risk-free, money-back guarantee.

Let your attendees know that you will refund their fees (or offer credit for next year) if they are dissatisfied and come forward to share the source of their dissatisfaction. Listen and ask the attendee what you can do to turn their dissatisfaction into satisfaction. In most cases, you can make a simple change to accommodate them and they will walk away happy. They will also be convinced that the organization really cares about meeting their needs.

49. Utilize awards and recognition as loyalty builders with your members, as well as with supplier communities.

Create an annual award delivery mechanism as a way to recognize and acknowledge the accomplishments and contributions to the organization of all member communities.

50. Create events to foster conventions in a virtual environment.

Utilize social networking tools to increase dialogue and gain traction for the topic at hand. If you don't have staff to manage this project, recruit a volunteer who is already using the tool.

51. Create "Early Bird" and "Night Owl" sessions.

With participants coming from different time zones, traditional workshop time blocks do not always correspond with attendee individual time clocks. Early Bird/Night Owl programming can provide an opportunity for those early risers or attendees who are more engaged later in the day. Introducing this flexibility into your education can be a positive experience and unique niche offering for your attendee base.

52. Examine your education sessions and identify ways to include a hands-on component.

Adults learn best by doing, but many workshops—general sessions in particular—are often passive learning experiences. To foster community outside the formal session environment while still promoting meaningful learning, offer a track of sessions that include small-group experiential learning opportunities. For example, offer a cooking class led by one of the hotel chefs followed by a discussion about the teamwork or planning lessons learned from cooking together. Get a local personal trainer to lead a fitness workshop and then have participants share their strategies for maintaining good work–life balance.

53. Implement a rigorous selection process for session topics and speakers.

Actively solicit session topics and speakers. Have each submission reviewed by four different reviewers in a blind review. Average the scores and determine a rating system to accept or reject submissions.

54. Let them feel the LOVE through APPLAUSE.

Provide a clap line for both attendees and exhibitors when your exhibit hall closes or conference ends. Recruit staff and volunteers to line up and thank both attendees and exhibitors as they leave the meeting. This show of appreciation through clapping, whistles, noise makers, and verbal expressions of thanks goes a long way with your audience and may cinch the deal in bringing them back next year.

Rethinking Event ROI: How Technology Can Save Live Events

The Participant Journey

The key to delivering better event experiences and creating better results lies in understanding, and monetizing, the participant journey. The journey around an event was simple. You invited members to an event, you delivered the event, and you followed up to see what your members thought. It was a simple model built around a few very productive days.

The only problem is that model doesn't meet the needs of participants. From members to sponsors to exhibitors, many events don't address the ways your participants want to participate.

What do your participants want?

They want more choices, increased relevance, and expanded interactivity. Put simply, your members and all your event participants want to engage with you and each other on their own terms.

That means in order to deliver better, more measureable results, event organizers need to stop thinking of live events as the destination and start thinking of them as steps in a journey to sustained community engagement.

To get there, associations need to leverage emerging technologies. The following is an overview of the four key areas of technology that event organizers are using to drive measurable ROI through community engagement.

1. Marketing Optimization

Target your market. Integrated email marketing tools allow organizers to reach out personally to members and provide important opportunities to sponsors and exhibitors. Through the use of advanced list segmentation, organizers can provide highly relevant and personalized messages to members. The result is happier members, higher attendance, and better results.

Look at the facts. Web analytics packages provide insight not only into the performance of your event website, but also important details like where members are abandoning the registration process and what webpages receive the most attention from your visitors. In the end, it allows organizers to react to the preferences of participants.

Turn members into promoters. Social sharing tools put the power of promotion in the hands of your audience. Members can see what friends are attending your events and even recommend your event to people who may want to attend. As marketing becomes less one-to-one and more one-to-many, organizers actually can spend less and drive more attendance.

2. Digital Interactivity

Go social. Event social networks and member communities are extending the lifecycle of events by providing a forum for interaction before, during, and after the event. Matching tools within these technologies can link members with each other, exhibitors, or sponsors based on desired outcomes from their experience. Members also can set up one-on-one meetings, build custom schedules, and discuss important topics.

Go mobile. Mobile event applications provide the full event experience from scheduling to networking to maps to paperless surveys in the palms of your members' hands. Plus, mobile organizer tools provide better insight into attendees, empowering exhibitors to connect with the right people at the right time.

Go virtual. Virtual events have proven to both increase attendance through online audiences and increase attendance at live events by adding value. Webcasting provides real-time, interactive access to sessions while virtual tradeshow tools allow virtual users to shop and interact with exhibitors and sponsors in a highly measurable environment.

3. Event Efficiency

Make it easy. Streamlined online registration platforms make it easy for participants to register for events and manage their preferences. Members can register for events and social networks in one smooth process. Speakers can submit papers for easy online voting. And exhibitors can choose space and select requirements. In the end, the experience is easy, the data is accurate, and participants are more satisfied.

Make it smooth. New onsite technologies have revolutionized the onsite experience. Offline self-service kiosks make check-in easy while removing the threat of internet downtime.

Track everything. Live experiences are increasingly easy to measure. Lead management tools go far beyond lead retrieval to provide detailed analytics on the performance of exhibitors against targets. Session scanning tools track continuing education units automatically while session access control makes sure prerequisites are met and session registrants get the seats they were promised.

4. Business Intelligence

It's not what they say, it's what they do. Event organizers have always been in the habit of asking participants what they thought. Now, business intelligence tools are allowing organizers to monitor the behavior of members to better target groups. For example, one technology company recently identified more than 200 leads that were in the buying cycle for a particular solution by studying session attendance trends at an event.

Get the whole story. In the past, event technology has been fragmented and mechanical. Integrated data warehousing has revolutionized the sophistication of intelligence around live experiences, providing a single, comprehensive view of the entire participant journey. This holistic, integrated approach to data management empowers organizers to analyze trends and drive value from every touch point with every participant.

A New Technology Standard

Changes in the participant journey have put new demands on association event organizers. Yet, those demands provide new opportunities. By implementing a new technology standard, events can reach farther, engage members longer, deliver more rich experiences, and create quantifiable results.

Live events don't have to be a poor communication channel. If association managers are listening to their participants—members, sponsors, and exhibitors—events will thrive, not just survive.

Excerpted from Olson, Eric. "Rethinking Event ROI: How Technology Can Save Live Events." *Meetings & Expositions,* November 2010.

REVENUE GENERATING AND COST SAVINGS

55. Brand conference bags.

When purchasing bags for your annual meeting, brand them with your organization logo instead of your meeting logo. This extends the life of the bag for the attendee and the likelihood of them using it throughout the year. Any additional bags can be used for future meetings and a large bulk buy can help with cost savings.

56. Partner with the destination CVB.

For pre- and post-event research and marketing, work together with the destination's Convention & Visitors Bureau (CVB). Utilize the CVB's complimentary services including attendee attitude surveys, analysis, marketing templates, fillers, and discounts. They can also provide access to their printer discounts, develop marketing collateral for your show, and create customized events for your attendees.

57. Supplement in-person events with online education.

To extend the value of your meetings, and to reach participants who are unwilling or unable to attend your face-to-face conferences, create an online educational program—in the form of webinars, an online training series, or webisodes—and charge a nominal fee for members to participate.

58. Promote exhibitor tutorials on the show floor.

Create an area on your exhibit hall floor where exhibitors can sign up for 10–15 minute presentations where they provide attendees with a tutorial on how to use their latest products/services. You can charge an additional fee to exhibitors for this enhanced exposure.

59. Provide sponsorship packages that bundle the benefits (and costs) of attendance, exhibiting, and sponsorship and generate increased visibility for the vendor.

Promote sponsorship packages such as

- 1st Level Package (Gold) which includes booth space, complimentary registration, logo on event site and in printed materials at event; and
- 2nd Level (Platinum/Diamond) which also allows sponsors to give a 1–2 minute introduction on their company prior to introducing a speaker.

You could also enhance their presence in the printed material with not only their logo, but also an advertisement or logo with a description of their products/services.

60. Develop a partnership with an alliance organization and host a joint event.

Partnering on a joint event enables cost savings on the venue and on marketing, and increases attendance by drawing members from both groups. (It also saves on expo and increases attendance through members not captured on both sides). Both organizations have an opportunity to capture additional members that may not have been members of both. Offering discounted memberships at the joint event may increase the opportunity to capture the new members and generate additional revenue.

61. "Buy early. Buy often. Buy more." Offer an incentive program for exhibitors via a points system.

Institute a points system that rewards exhibitors for signing up early, registering as a return exhibitor, and taking increased space—which in turn expands floors and provides a better show experience for attendees. Tracking points for exhibitors thanks and recognizes the companies that support your floor the most.

62. Encourage exhibitors to purchase more space to sell out a floor.

Return exhibitors or new exhibitors seeking to make a splash on the floor can be incentivized to buy more space. A way to implement such an idea would be volume square footage discounts. For example, buy one 10×10 space and get your second 10×10 space for 50 percent off.

63. Consider in-kind sponsorships instead of monetary contributions.

Help take dollars off your bottom line by creating in-kind sponsorships with conference items such as, bags, lanyards, décor, etc.

64. Implement a pre-conference and onsite branding campaign for key partners.

Visual campaigns linking partners to the power of the organization brand can yield great exposure and elicit even greater support and goodwill from companies. Staff should provide reporting on the effectiveness of the campaign on partner recall and identification ramping up to, during, and after a show. Simple surveying and personalized reporting can be a valuable and sellable outcome.

65. Sell "Complete Exhibitor Packages" (CEP) at various price points to include key marketing, sales, and logistics opportunities.

Offer various levels of "complete exhibitor packages" (CEP) to address a variety of exhibitor show objectives. The packages could include exhibit space, banners, furnishing, registration, virtual show presence, sponsorship of an event, association publication, etc. This would save time in the sales and service area, as well as help your corporate partners increase their success at your show.

66. Convert paper handouts to digital to go green.

Transition from paper to CD or web-based handouts. It saves money and trees, and demonstrates your commitment to protecting the environment. Seek sponsorship for this creative new distribution channel.

67. Establish a buyer-seller opportunity for attendees and exhibitors.

Solicit your membership to participate in a needs assessment that applies to the supplier community, and share the findings of the needs assessment with members. Your association, thereafter, can facilitate a connection between buyers (members) and sellers (suppliers) at an established cost.

68. Offer unique tours of the destination.

Partner with local convention and visitors' bureaus to secure complimentary tours of the city. Charge attendees a fee for this unique experience.

69. Maximize the tradeshow's exhibitor impact during the meeting.

Communicate the value of the tradeshow to attendees through newsletters and "how to" websites. This helps exhibitors learn more about the attendees and how to best interact. Create specific gatherings for exhibitors with key association staff and leadership.

70. Divide the annual operating budget for your meeting into profit centers.

Set a net profit goal for each profit center plus 2–3 tiers above the goal. Pay bonuses based on which tier your staff achieves beyond the goal.

71. Require attendees to book inside the block in order to ride conference shuttles.

Upon confirmation of registration, compare the housing list with the registration list. Contact those outside of the block prior to the meeting to purchase their transportation pass. Identify attendees outside of the block with a different color badge.

72. Negotiate a bulk purchase of speaker books to be given onsite to attendees at the lecture or via a book signing.
Obtaining quality speakers can be expensive, but in cases where a speaker is published, an alternative may be available as opposed to lecture charges. Helping the speaker to sell additional books benefits the speaker, but provides an attendee benefit as well. The added value to all participants can be significant and it can also potentially offset expenses.

73. Target relative, but not represented, vendors to sell out your show floor.
Look at your list of sponsors and exhibitors and see what types of valid companies are missing. Open your phone book and start making calls. Telling a company directly that you need their type of business represented on your floor will pique their interest. Also, ask attendees to personally invite vendors they would like to see at your show.

74. Develop an online leadership toolkit.
Create an online leadership/influencers toolkit that the Board of Directors, committees, volunteers, speakers, exhibitors, and sponsors can use to spread the word about their involvement in the meeting and also invite people to attend. This will open up your meeting to potential attendees who may not be on your direct mail or email lists. Invitations will come from a respected source, which should result in increased awareness of the meeting and increased attendance from new audiences.

75. Offer offsite activities as a value add-on to registration.
Select sites and hosts who can offer tours and demonstrations of a particular technology or activity. Have services donated when possible, but charge a fee for attendees. Tours can be determined based on participant needs assessment, conference theme, or current issues or trends. Train volunteers to travel with each group and facilitate conversation and learning during the travel to and from the site. Provide a reflection and application worksheet for people to complete after the tour, noting interesting things they saw or learned and how they might apply them in their own settings.

76. Create a LinkedIn account for your company that requires active membership to join.

Let membership leads come to you. Verify that anyone requesting to join your LinkedIn page is a member before allowing them to join your organization's page. If they are not a member, send them membership information and let them know they must be a member to join.

77. Add large LCD or plasma screens to your Expo Hall for added advertising revenue.

Use a large screen to act as a jumbotron at your event. It's a great place for you to display important messages to attendees, but also a great spot to sell advertising and recognize key sponsors.

78. Create "Sense of Place" or "Identity" lounges in your expo hall or meeting.

Create meeting spaces within the expo hall or around the venue that can be built out by exhibiting companies and/or sponsors to help deliver brand awareness or an enhanced experience to attendees. Examples of the lounges and their design can be provided along with guidelines. Price these lounges at a lower cost than your booth space, and offer them to your exhibitors and sponsors as a benefit. The exhibitor or sponsor would decorate this space to communicate their brand. You have created an additional visibility opportunity for your suppliers, created a new revenue stream, and added to the networking area/lounges for attendees at a profit to you.

79. Offer exhibitors the option to purchase floor banners that can bring visibility and additional revenue.

Offer exhibitors the option to purchase floor banners to help drive traffic to their booth. You have seen these floor banners/stickers in your grocery store promoting the latest snack food. You can design the template for the floor banners to help them visualize the look and feel, and you should identify on the floor plan the locations for the banners. Then the exhibitors can select the location and the look they want within the parameters you specify.

80. Turn exhibitor giveaways and prizes into auction items.
Ask your exhibitors if they are willing to donate their giveaways as auction items. It's a win-win for both, as you can help promote them and their prize as well as benefit from the money your members are willing to pay for the prizes.

81. Produce meeting materials in the city where you are hosting your meeting.
Onsite meeting materials (i.e., printed schedule of events, printed tradeshow floor maps, education white papers/handouts [either in print or CD-ROM], etc.) are costly. Considering options for locally producing these materials may equal savings. Vendors you have a long-term contract with to create these products may have subcontractors in the meeting area who can print the materials; and area CVBs or Chambers of Commerce may be able to identify local companies to assist with production if you are currently free of vendor obligations. Local vendors may be capable of delivering materials across town at a fraction of the cost, whereas your usual vendor would charge you big money to ship over a long distance. These savings can contribute to a healthy bottom line for your event.

82. Negotiate hotel rebates which can help offset some meeting costs.
When negotiating hotel contracts, consider building in a small hotel rebate per room occupied per night to help offset shuttle or additional meeting cost that may be specific to a city or your meeting. These rebates need to be negotiated before the contract is signed and your organization should be transparent with your members that, for example, $5 of their room rate goes towards the meeting transportation or whatever it is being used for.

83. Cut your beverage expenses by providing reusable containers to attendees.
Think about providing a reuseable container to attendees and providing water coolers around the convention center instead of bottles of water. This can drastically cut your beverage expense, especially over several days of a meeting, and it goes a long way to greening your meeting.

84. Protect your meeting's reputation and recover losses due to unforeseen incidents by purchasing event cancellation insurance.

Regardless of the nature of your event (i.e., tradeshow, annual congress, educational conference, etc.), insurance against cancellation, interruption, or postponement can act as a buffer against things that may unexpectedly affect your meeting. Although we can't always predict or avoid natural and manmade disasters, insurance provides a way to recoup losses and mitigate damages that result from them. Policies can be customized to fit the needs of your specific meeting, and the cost of insurance is often a fraction of the expenses you would incur should unfortunate circumstances impact your event.

85. Sell a transportation sponsorship to and from the local airport.

Attendees will appreciate this gesture and sponsors can get visibility without outside bus banners/wraps, head rest covers, promotional materials on the bus, etc.

86. Offer a "wow" experience.

Secure complimentary services from the destination that would provide an unforgettable, "wow" experience, such as a wine-making class in Napa or a "learn to surf" day trip. Charge a fee for this unique experience.

87. Offer volunteer opportunities.

Work with a local non-profit to secure volunteer opportunities so attendees can make a meaningful contribution to the organization. Charge a fee with a portion of the proceeds going directly to the charitable organization and the remainder covering costs and generating revenue for your association.

88. Add registration sponsorship tables.

Enhance your registration experience by adding sponsorship tables to your registration area. Sponsors pay a fee to have a table and get added exposure.

89. Create post-show offerings for sponsors or exhibitors for a specific fee.

Create value-added offerings for sponsors or exhibitors. Determine what's important to both groups and add a post-show offer. Sell an electronic and final list of attendees to vendors that exhibited or to potential future vendors.

90. Solicit a sponsor for your attendee binders/program books.

Offer sponsorship opportunities to provide binders/program books at registration. Each attendee gets a copy, giving great visibility to your sponsor.

91. Sell key card, door drop, and newspaper sponsorships.

Make sure that you have written into your hotel contracts that they will not charge you a fee for these sponsorship opportunities. Negotiate complimentary newspaper delivery with your venue and then offer a newspaper bag sponsorship to your vendors.

92. Offer transportation passes.

Negotiate reduced transportation fees or transportation rebates with the city or venue. However, charge a minimum fee to attendees who can purchase the transportation pass while registering. Consider also having the registration passes sponsored and include the sponsor's logo on the pass.

93. Use local talent for entertainment.

Hire talent that is local to the community where your meeting is taking place. Ask the local members, CVB, or hotel to make suggestions. Consider lowering your cost by using a DJ for social events rather than hiring a band.

94. Sponsor first-time attendees.

Offer vendors the opportunity to sponsor a first-time attendee. This will provide the organization an opportunity to capture revenue as well as enhancing the experience for an attendee who may otherwise have been unable to attend.

95. Sell the opportunity for exhibitors to have their logo drawn in chalk outside the convention center entrance and sell floor decals to a sponsor.

Meeting attendees will work with an artist to help them draw their sponsor logo on the walkway leading up to the convention center. You can also secure a sponsor for floor decals to spread throughout the conference space. For example: footprints with logos, directional arrows with logos, etc.

96. Sell meeting space to vendors or affiliate companies who wish to meet during your event.

Sell your contracted complimentary meeting rooms that you aren't using to vendors or affiliates for product demonstrations, receptions, dinners, committee meetings, etc.

97. Create breakouts that require an additional fee to attend.

Design specialized breakouts, such as a cooking class that focuses on leadership skills or an activity breakout that shows you how to design team building events. Charge an additional fee for these premium programs.

98. Use local volunteers instead of a temporary staffing company.

Using local volunteers will help you save on labor costs. Plus, they are a great asset to your welcome or information desks as they know the local area.

99. Charge premiums for exhibit booths located around your key traffic drivers.

Consider offering free exhibit space to exhibitors who are known to be good attendance drivers. Then charge the exhibitors who pick space around them a premium.

100. Sell exhibitors and sponsors access to in-house local TV channels.

Negotiate low- or no-cost access to the channels within the hotel. Provide exclusive access to this promotional vehicle to exhibitors and sponsors as a way to reach attendees in their hotel rooms. Develop an easy process for connecting the approved advertiser with the appropriate contact at the hotel. You will raise revenue and limit access to non-approved advertisers.

101. Reduce attrition risk by requiring sub-block agreements with affiliates and exhibitors.

Establish a protocol of requiring a written agreement with exhibitors and affiliates who hold blocks of rooms. Include language that holds them responsible for any attrition that results from their cancellation or failure to pickup rooms.

102. Offer a lounge and special benefits for attendees to buy into.

Create a visible, high-profile lounge area with comfortable seating, WiFi, snacks, and beverages. Sell access similar to an airline club. You can add benefits that might attract your attendees and adjust the price point to work for your group.

103. Keep contractor costs fair by going out to bid periodically.

Even when you are happy with your vendor relationships and the services they provide, discipline yourself to go out to bid. Giving yourself the chance to review proposals and assess the competition can save your organization big dollars.

104. Control room reset, AV, and labor costs by establishing a standard room set.

Determine the best meeting room and audio visual set for each meeting room that can work throughout the meeting. Inform all speakers, committee chairs, and staff ahead of time and help them work with the set to accomplish their objectives. This will limit the need for expensive and time-consuming room resets.

105. Benchmark registration, exhibit, and sponsorship pricing to ensure your prices are competitive.

When setting any price or fee, do competitive research online to gather pricing from other meetings that your members attend. Review your pricing to ensure it is competitive. Build a multiyear price strategy to increase or decrease accordingly.

106. Sell private meeting room space on the show floor.
Create a private space on the tradeshow floor where exhibitors can take clients to have more in-depth conversations, sign contracts, and close deals. Charge a nominal fee for exhibitors, vendors, and sponsors to have access to this area.

107. Sell "buy one, get one" promotions (bogos) and public logo projections to your sponsors.
Contract with convention centers, hotels, and event space to utilize vibrant lighting and bogo effects. Sponsor recognitions using these effects are dynamic, attractive, and don't cost a lot. This provides an opportunity to sell high traffic areas to suppliers while creating a visually stunning atmosphere.

108. Include membership fee in meeting registration to incentivize renewal and encourage attendance.
Create pricing packages to include annual membership fee together with your meeting registration that represents a lower cost than the non-member fee.

109. Require exhibitors to book inside the block or stay at headquarter hotels in order to receive the exhibitor packet and to confirm booth space.
Exhibitors must book within the block or at the headquarter hotel prior to securing exhibit space. This ensures a certain percentage of guest rooms picked up in your block.

110. Go beyond your current sponsorship menu and simply ask.
Ask potential sponsors what it is they would like to sponsor. The ideas that you hear may increase your sponsorship potential and provide innovative services to your attendees.

111. Consider opening up your silent auction bidding.
Why limit your silent auction to only your members and attendees? Consider posting fundraising auction items on the association/ meeting website and also on eBay or other public sites. It could increase your income and sponsoring donors' exposure. Be sure to check laws and regulations in your state.

112. Look within your organization to ensure appropriate departments or divisions are resourced.

Is there potential for your for-profit subsidiary to financially support your meeting? Are other departments held accountable for spending and budgets during the convention? Sometimes the most effective cost-saving measure is to refine your existing budget and expenditures.

113. Look to your vendor base to help defray costs for your combined customers.

Many meeting suppliers also receive revenue streams from the meeting attendees or exhibitors. Ask them to help pay for services provided to their customers. For example, your drayage firm could help sponsor the Exhibitor Lounge.

114. Evaluate what level of costs are really needed for a keynote speaker.

Most attendees do not attend to hear the keynote speaker only. Do you need a $100,000 speaker when a $10,000 one might do?

115. Consider an awards reception versus an awards banquet.

An awards reception will be less costly than a banquet. In addition, attendees will have a greater opportunity to interact with each other and mingle.

116. Sell sponsorships for both online and print meeting magazines and inserts for conference tote bags and/or registration packets.

Sponsorship of these opportunities creates high visibility opportunities for businesses to reach attendees with their information.

117. Send continuing education letters and certificates electronically.

This will save postage costs and attendees will now have an electronic copy that they can save for future use with their respective state licensing boards.

118. Use hotels with various price points.
This will allow more attendees the opportunity to stay within the blocks. This benefits the association's hotel block total and allows those attendees who are more price conscious to participate.

119. Review and audit F&B and AV verifications.
In your post-con evaluation, did you utilize all that you ordered? Could you have saved and can you tighten your process for next year?

120. Create a peer group within your industry to brainstorm potential revenue generators/cost savings.
Bring together your brightest volunteer minds to help you brainstorm different revenue streams for your convention.

121. Find out who exhibitors want to be near or far from.
Often exhibitors want to be far away from each other. Allowing them to choose space away from their competition increases their satisfaction, but you can also use the list to identify new prospects that might not be exhibiting with you.

122. Use sponsors as subject matter experts to create content while generating revenue.
Include sponsors and key stakeholders of programs as subject matter experts to help shape and participate in generating program content while increasing your revenue. This allows for a strong return on investment for your sponsor and partner. However, be sure they know they must provide content, not a commercial.

123. Sell conference recordings.
Work with a vendor to record the conference sessions for sale to attendees, especially if there are multiple tracks/sessions at the same time.

124. Create a "you have my ear" program.
Create a program where association members are willing to meet with suppliers for 5–10 minutes. Suppliers would pay a fee to register. Association members just agree to listen. They may learn

something new about each other. Offer your members incentives to listen, such as free access to a reception or session handouts.

125. Sell a "new product showcase" feature of your meeting.

Sell access to a special showcase of products released recently or about to be released. Promote to attendees and provide a high-profile location.

126. Contract with hotel or convention center to waive parking fees and allow you to sell packages instead.

Use your relationships and negotiation skills to obtain parking space rights. If a property will redirect parking revenue to your organization, you can resell it as attendee parking packages. These contract stipulations can generate a great deal of revenue for meetings capitalizing on commuter and short–drive-time attendees.

127. Consider tax status in site selection.

Your 501(c)(3) organization may be exempt from taxes in certain states. Know your tax status and file for exemption when possible. Use this information to evaluate potential sites.

128. Ask members and attendees to identify products and companies they want to see at your exhibit.

Your members are a great source of leads for building your exhibit and sponsorship programs. Ask them annually to provide information on the products they use and need, then market to those companies. Reach out to new prospects with data that show that their current and potential customers want to see them at your show.

Boost Your Tradeshow Revenue with New Digital Tools

Following are a few examples of how some associations and event managers are making today's technology deliver more revenue and value for them and all of their stakeholders.

Online Booths/Packages

Ten, even five years ago, getting exhibitors to purchase online booths was a tough sell. Getting them to go one step further and invest in upgrades for their online booths such as additional product categories, show specials, and product pages was next to impossible.

But Google and other online search engines and advertising tools have changed all that. Today, just like Google, show organizers such as the Automotive Aftermarket Products Expo, World of Concrete/Hanley-Wood, and the American Industrial Hygiene Association are making substantial revenue with exhibitors that want better online search tools on show websites, combined with enhanced online booths that feature more information about their products and services for buyers.

Potential revenue: An average show with 225 exhibitors can realistically generate $10,000, $25,000, and $35,000+ in the first, second, and third years (respectively) of launching an online booth program—more than enough to pay for the program in the first year.

Context-Sensitive Session Sponsorships

Similar to buying AdWords on Google, when members and attendees go to your event website and search for education sessions at your conference by keyword, subject, or track, one or more sponsors related to the session subject can appear in the right-hand margin of the search results. This gives exhibitors added exposure and visibility to a highly qualified audience—just like with Google.

Potential revenue: Online sponsorships for the average 24–30 session conference can generate $15,000, $30,000, and $50,000 in the first three years, respectively.

Networking and Matchmaking Systems

Popular consumer marketplace websites like MySpace and YouTube have helped familiarize members/attendees and exhibitors in recent years with online matchmaking and networking tools and how they can be used in the business world, before, during, and after events. Exhibitors have always wanted more opportunities to network and connect with high-quality buyers at shows. And, similar to preshow registration lists (but much better), now you can match them up with only the attendees that are interested in their products, resulting in a lot less waste on printing, paper, postage, and time. Similar to how you have sold your registration lists for preshow mailings, you can now sell these better-qualified matches and appointment opportunities with highly qualified attendee/buyers.

Potential revenue: Give exhibitors a starter package of a half-dozen appointments with their best matches, then offer them packages of 25, 50, and 100 appointments at $250, $375, and $500, respectively. The potential revenue for the average show can be $10,000, $25,000, and $35,000+ in the first three years, respectively.

More Revenue Opportunities

Following is a list of more online revenue tools:

- Rotating banner ads (revenue potential: $10,000–50,000+, first year)
- Exhibitor logo in online booth ($50–200 per exhibitor)
- Exhibitor logo on floor plan ($200–1,000 per exhibitor)
- Multiple product pages ($100+ per page)
- New product showcase ($250–500 per exhibitor)
- Press release pages ($25+ per page)
- Show specials pages ($100+ per page)
- Enhanced online booth profile (additional word count, $50+)
- Premium listing in exhibitor list ($100+)

Combinations

Depending on what you feel you can launch successfully the first year and beyond, you can offer your exhibitors just one of the programs above or a combination of two or more.

Potential revenue: $35,000–100,000+ in additional revenue by the third year, plus enhanced online visibility, increased at-show booth traffic, better quality leads, and more sales for your exhibitors.

All of that, in turn, should lead to happier exhibitors, lower attrition rates, more space sales, and new revenue for your show, exhibitors, and association.

Excerpted from: Hatch, Michael J. "Boost Your Tradeshow Revenue With New Digital Tools." *Meetings & Expositions,* May 2008.

ATTENDANCE BUILDING

129. Add a "Bring a Partner" component to your meeting.
Encourage your attendees to bring a colleague—identify appropriate partners who can benefit by attending together (i.e., bring your boss, your staff, a vendor, a specific member of their management team).

130. Increase attendance using webinars.
Use webinars or videos on your conference website to give "teaser" presentations to help increase and promote attendance at future events.

131. Make it easy for potential attendees to get approval to attend using a "justification kit."
Provide potential attendees with a kit to help them talk about the value of your meeting in advance, in order for them to justify the time and money to their organizations.

132. Capitalize on the attraction of poster/research submissions.
Posters and research submissions, such as food locations and prize giveaways, can draw traffic. Strategically placing these programs in areas of the hall where additional traffic is desired for strategic purposes is a worthy effort.

133. Utilize research programming to engage students and foster loyalty for future years as well.

Do not underestimate the power of poster presentations. Significantly increasing the number of poster presentations and standardizing the format may lead to the following benefits: (1) increasing conference attendance, (2) increasing the number of speakers who are funded to attend conferences, (3) increasing interaction between speakers and attendees, and (4) integrating students into their professional conference.

134. Package your registrations to include key attendees.

Provide 2-for-1 registrations for key attendees to make it possible for companies or organizations to bring more staff to your event. For example, offer a package deal where executive directors or CEOs who register for a conference are allowed to register one of their meeting planners for free. Target a segment that normally does attend and offer to them that if they register they can bring their staff professional (the person you are trying to attract from an organization) at no charge.

135. Market/brand a segment of a program to prospective local/regional attendees.

Group special programming and/or offer programming at a special registration rate for potential consumers within a targeted market (i.e., three-hour drive time) to increase attendance.

136. Promote international attendance by making the visa process easy and affordable for prospective attendees.

Offer support from the national organization to prospective international attendees by providing links on the registration website to affordable visa processing.

137. Add the blogging/Twitter community to your events media lists.

Treat the blogging and Twitter community like press, giving them opportunities to meet with speakers and/or authors in advance. They are always looking for content and will promote or give visibility to your meetings to their followers or community.

138. Nurture attendance at regional and chapter events to build momentum and attendance in the national events.

The national organization should provide marketing and programming support to improve the attendance of the local events, help grow membership of the chapters, and more clearly articulate the value of attending the national event.

139. Partner with other organizations to cross promote.

Partner with other organizations at no cost to them or you. Give them exposure at your meeting and in your marketing (brochures, website, magazine, email, e-newsletter, etc.) in return for their promoting your meeting through their own communications outlets. This will help broaden your marketing reach to potential new prospects or attendees. Make sure that the agreement is in writing and that the visibility is structured so both parties feel they are getting equal benefit and value.

140. Utilize the power of your members to extend your reach to potential new audiences.

Train your board, committees, volunteers, speakers, exhibitors, and sponsors to use social media to get the word out and reward them for doing so. By encouraging audiences that are engaged with your organization to spread the word about your organization and your events, you can achieve increased awareness of your organization, increased attendance at meetings, and increased sales of products and services.

141. Offer a discounted registration for all attendees who attend this year as an incentive to attend next year.

Motivating return attendees onsite can free up promotional resources among staff to solicit new attendees. Set a deadline for this discount before registration rates increase.

142. Create a marketing campaign using social media to engage the younger generation and promote your annual meeting.

Make use of all social media tools to educate younger members on targeted aspects of your event. Set up a Facebook event page to engage younger attendees in a focus group regarding meeting expectations. This is a good way to easily encourage participation of a hard-to-reach audience.

143. Recognize that international growth can make up for lost members and convention revenues from the recent recession.

Opportunities for expanding international participation in meetings are high and can be enhanced easily through electronic media. Work with international agents and members to do marketing and outreach in their respective countries. They have a network of potential registrants and can provide outreach and targeted messages in their native languages.

144. Partner with the destination marketing organization (CVB) of the host city to promote attendance.

Work with the destination marketing organization (DMO) (CVB) of the host city to promote attendance. Have a table at the event, manned by the DMO, to promote attendance at next year's event. Have a link to the DMO on the event registration webpage. Set up a booth or table onsite at the event to promote local shopping, dining, and attraction options. Meet with CVB representatives early to take full advantage of all the resources they can offer to promote and enhance your event. Their partnerships can even extend your marketing budgets.

145. Engage business partners to help promote your event through social media and viral marketing.

Engage alliance associations, exhibitors, and committees to promote your event. Create an international marketing strategy that creates value for both the association and the partners. Promotional opportunity creates association value and exposure.

146. Develop a process for attendees to create and share ideas to increase attendance at the event.

Provide space for attendees to share ideas on a registration forum. Design an event site to allow for idea sharing. Recognize those attendees who come up with winning ideas.

147. Create a student advocacy program for the event.

Design a program that works directly with the universities to allow credit and excused absences for attending conferences. Provide complimentary transportation to and from school to the convention. Waive registration fees to engage student members and foster mentorship opportunities.

148. Develop an online influencer's toolkit.

Develop an online leadership and influencer's toolkit that board and committee members, volunteers, speakers, exhibitors, and sponsors can use to spread the word about their involvement in the meeting and invite people to attend. Make it simple so volunteers can reach out to their contacts easily to help get the word out in a grassroots manner to help build awareness and attendance.

149. Create online registration software that offers a reduced registration fee if lodging at the headquarter hotel is reserved.

Design registration software to recognize lodging reservations at the headquarter hotel. Offering a reduced registration incentive helps keep attendance at the headquarter hotel.

150. Create a marketing initiative that utilizes photos and testimonials of conference attendees.

Engage members to submit testimonials and photos via free tools like Flickr. Create engagement and connection through this kind of member involvement. Members will enjoy seeing their photos and quotes in your newsletter and in future promotional materials.

151. Create an incentive program for attendees to visit your sponsors.

Have attendees visit exhibitors deserving of greater traffic or under-trafficked areas of the floor to check-in and register to win a giveaway.

152. Provide exhibitors with a promotional code to distribute to their customers.

Codes can provide incentives for attendees such as discounted registration or a reception funded by exhibitors in the exhibit hall.

The code will allow show management to track promotion back to specific exhibitors.

153. Build attendance by marketing to potential attendees in the region near the meeting site.

Purchase lists of potential attendees that live within driving range of the meeting site. Conduct e-blasts and send direct mail to these potential attendees.

154. Design graphics for attendees, speakers, and exhibitors that allow them to promote their participation in your event.

Create "I'm Exhibiting," "I'm Speaking," "I'm Attending" graphics that attendees, speakers, and exhibitors can use on their websites, blogs, Facebook pages, etc., to help promote your meeting.

155. Support unemployed members by offering networking and employment services at the event.

Provide coaching sessions, resumé writing, and counseling to unemployed members. A fee could be charged or a sponsor could support this initiative, providing both money to the organization and a service to members.

156. Capitalize on pre-show social media.

Run a status campaign where volunteers and exhibitors update their status on Facebook and LinkedIn to reflect that they are going and what their booth number is so that their communities hear about your meeting. This expands the promotional factor for a show beyond efforts of the organization and broadens the reach of exhibitor influence.

157. Target marketing works.

Start collecting data on your attendees and use it to your advantage. Push out email with targeted content that addresses their specific needs. Create print pieces for certain segments highlighting what's in it for them. For example, email all of the attorneys with a subject line that features the attorney speaker.

158. Invite your speakers to Tweet the event before the actual conference begins.

Most meetings now have a hash tag—that information should be communicated to registrants as they register so they begin to use it before the meeting. This will help spread the word about the meeting from a more grassroots level rather than communication only coming from the organization.

159. Start a viral marketing campaign.

Make it easy for members, attendees, speakers, and exhibitors to pass on your marketing and promotions to their colleagues and supplier partners. Set up a "forward this message" approach on your website. You can offer prizes to motivate and generate excitement, but most of all, be sure to thank them for their referrals.

160. Create a web-based RFP system for association members where successful usage results in credits for future events.

Engage members in utilizing a web-based RFP process. Members are rewarded for utilizing your supplier members. The association benefits as members receive credit for meeting registration.

161. Provide free registration passes to each booth space.

Exhibitors can invite buyers/clients to the meeting to visit them in the exhibit hall. Guests can bring their special registration pass to the onsite registration area to receive their hall pass for that day.

162. Use member experiences to demonstrate the meeting value.

Share short stories about members and their experiences at your meeting, highlighting the attendees' takeaways. Have the stories vary in the type of experience (i.e., new ideas gained at the meeting, connection with like professionals for idea sharing and problem solving, solutions discovered, etc.). Use these stories in your marketing (i.e., brochures, website, Tweets, audio testimonials, etc.).

163. Implement an attendee referral program.

Catch the wave on attendees' enthusiasm and build into your registration a referral opportunity. Provide attendees an incentive and an opportunity to give the organization names and email addresses of people they feel would benefit from attending the meeting. You can brand it with something catchy like "Be part of the BUZZ." Provide gift cards to a well known coffee house in exchange for referral names. You can increase the value with the number of names—5 names, a $5 gift card; 10 names, a $10 gift card. You can get a message printed on the card holder and order the cards in bulk. Then mail the cards out to those that participated. Attendees are amazed at the follow-up and will continue to spread the good word.

164. Provide exhibitors with a pre-written press release.

In your exhibitor service kit, include a fill-in-the-blank press release that allows exhibitors to quickly and easily promote their participation in your event.

165. Use quotes from post-show evaluations as promotion for next year's show.

Skim your post-show evaluations for good quotes concerning your conference. Contact the person who submitted the quote to see if they are willing to lend their quote and name to promotional material for next year's show. Do post-show follow up with both those who attended and those who did not. For those who didn't, be sure to convey that they missed something significant. Be sure to include your future meeting dates in your follow up.

166. Capture testimonials at the event to market future events.

There is nothing better than word of mouth from industry practitioners sharing their experiences and verbalizing the value of your meeting to their peers. So plan on capturing video at your next event with key audiences. Set up a room, designate a specific day, and recruit attendees ahead of time to participate.

167. Post all conference marketing material on your website.

Place electronic copies of your flyers, program books, etc., on your website. Inevitably, you've missed hitting some key people or audiences in your mailers. By posting these pieces on your website, those you missed can benefit from viewing the pieces on demand.

168. Have attendees write a self-addressed letter explaining what they learned at your event and how they plan to implement it.
Remind attendees of how valuable your conference was by having them write a letter to themselves stating what takeaways they got and action plans for the future. Mail the letters to them along with registration information for next year's show.

169. Post daily highlight videos during the show.
Hire a conference video company or capture event highlights using a simple home camera with video capabilities. Post daily highlights on your site to entice those who weren't able to make this year's show to register next year.

170. Offer scholarships to meetings for qualified attendees.
Affording registration, housing, or travel scholarships can increase attendance and improve customer satisfaction while building loyalty to your meeting's brand. Scholarship candidates could be attendees with lower-tier income or small organizational budgets, as well as students and emerging professionals. If an individual or organization is experiencing hard times, reaching out to them with a scholarship, whether applied to a specific attendance use or provided via a general reimbursement of expenses, may be rewarded by return attendance when their situation turns around. Similarly, engaging students, younger members, or attendees new to the profession can be the start of a wonderful relationship. These attempts to reduce attendee costs can do wonders for building educational participation and tradeshow traffic. You might target key sponsors or partners to lower rates in relation to the services they provide in connection to the meeting, such as hotel stays and flights, as part of a bulk discount package or in-kind support of the event. However you choose to provide aid to attendees by reducing their overhead for attending your meeting, you will likely reap benefits in both the short-term and long-term.

171. Generate energy and excitement on the show floor by conducting booth contests.
Engaging attendees in booth judging is a great way to encourage interactions with exhibitors. Consider using first-time attendees as

your booth judges. They'll have a fresh perspective of the booths and it's a great way to encourage them to visit the tradeshow floor, which can be intimidating.

172. Provide an extensive write-up of accessibility issues on your website.

Providing this information will allow attendees with disabilities to know beforehand what to expect. The more comprehensive, the better! Include such information as what type of accommodations are in the individual rooms, public restrooms, and nearest green space for service animals.

173. Work with a trade publication to promote your event.

Trade publications or other media outlets can provide coverage of your event, before, during, and after. Offer them incentives such as free booth space and complimentary registrations to attend.

174. Offer free registration if an attendee agrees to meet with a predetermined number of vendors.

If an event has vendors, this is a great way to make sure they receive quality leads and time with attendees and provides attendees with a means to attend if funds are tight.

175. Have registration companies incorporate links to registrants' social media networks.

Have your registration company link with registrants' social media/personal contacts (Outlook) network to send an email to their identified friends and colleagues saying "I am attending X conference, you should too!" with a link to register.

176. Create niche programming and market specifically to those audiences.

Develop programs for each subgroup within your conference (such as students, new professionals, CEOs, etc.). Send targeted marketing to each group promoting the programming that you developed just for them.

177. Create a chapter challenge.
Have each chapter market the event and provide an incentive (such as educational resources, gift cards, etc.) for the chapter with the highest percentage of their members attending.

178. Give attendees the ability to sign a banner showing they attended.
Create a large banner with a map of the United States or the world. Have attendees sign their name or put a push pin in the area they are from. Post the finished map on your website so people can see which states were most represented or under-represented.

179. Create a hosted buyer program.
Work with exhibitors and sponsors to create a hosted buyer program. Have a qualification process and minimum number of appointments and/or interactions that a hosted buyer must have in order to stay on a hosted basis.

180. Create and send out save-the-date mailers as well as e-blasts.
It is important to get your dates on your potential attendee's calendar for annual events. Send it one month after the previous year's event with a follow-up two months later. For a luncheon or smaller event, send your save-the-date promotion at least three months prior to the event. For email promotions, add hyperlinks that put the event on their Outlook calendar.

181. Hand out promotional pieces at your current meeting with the dates and logo for your next meeting.
Create different types of promotional pieces that include the dates and logo of the next meeting to hand out at your current meeting. Examples: post-it-notes, coasters, coffee mugs—anything that an attendee would use frequently.

182. Create a call for papers and encourage more attendees to become presenters.
Develop a component to your educational program that allows for your member experts to present on various topics. Start the call for

papers at least ten months prior to the meeting. Encourage selected presenters to invite attendees as well.

183. Create a special price structure for meeting attendance.
Offer a special price for students, unemployed member or young professionals, as well as for first-time attendees. An introductory price may help get them interested in the organization. The special price can be set for one meeting or for purchase of a series of three or four programs. Make it a limited-time offer.

184. Be sure value is conveyed.
Create verbiage that describes what they will get out of attending. The more expensive the program, the more details needed. Provide a contact person they can speak to if more information is needed.

185. Create a sense of urgency—You don't want to miss out!
Let attendees know space is limited and filling up quickly. Send out updates on registration, perhaps even listing some people who have recently signed up to attend.

186. Invite people to attend meetings personally.
Have staff, board members, and committee members call prospective members or members that have not yet registered for a meeting and encourage them to attend the meeting. People are more likely to participate if invited personally.

187. Print an article in your newsletter or journal one month prior to the meeting highlighting timely topics to be presented.
If there is an especially hot/important topic that you want meeting attendees to know about, promote it in an article that will appear in your journal or newsletter just prior to your meeting.

188. Print promotional materials in multiple languages.
Distribute the materials when attending or exhibiting at international meetings to show the international members you care about them enough to promote your meeting in their language.

189. Post video messages on your webpage about the meeting and its location.

Ask your speakers to do a quick tease video. Have your meeting planner talk about the meeting location highlights, what to expect when you are there, etc. Have your education director give highlights of certain sessions that will be presented. Ask the CVB in your city to create or provide a video about the meeting location. This helps build excitement about the program and the city. Build anticipation over several months by offering hints or clues about a particularly intriguing topic. Let prospective attendees know that the full topic will be disclosed at the meeting.

190. Offer a complimentary registration to local members in exchange for one day of volunteer service at your meeting.

Include local members at the meeting by assigning them tasks such as introducing speakers; provide them with a one-day or full complimentary registration in exchange for their help and services.

191. Make your email campaign edgy.

Promote your meeting to members and nonmembers with an email campaign—but, make it simple, sparse, and edgy. Use a concise message and effective images, and do not include too many details. Send short, easy-to-read messages to create excitement. Use consistent brand logo and lots of white space.

192. Create a "local leaders" program to expand internationally.

Have U.S.-based "leaders" extend formal invitations to peers in other countries. Show the clear benefits of participation, and build relationships that can be nurtured in person at your event. Reaching out to international colleagues creates a feeling of trust, much like the old "pen pal" philosophy.

193. Create a partnership with the hotel to develop incentives to generate early-bird registrations.

Offer a free stay at the hotel (either before or after the conference or at a future time). Work with hotel to offer discounts at restaurants, shops, or even the spa. Those registered prior to the early-bird cutoff date are eligible to win.

194. Create an Ambassadors program.
Have a volunteer group of ambassadors identify potential new attendees. Reach out to them with a formal invitation to attend and offer a commitment to walk them through the decision-making and registration process. Offer to meet up with them onsite to show them the ropes and immerse them as an attendee.

195. Use your photographer and videographer to help promote the meeting and create excitement.
Have your photographer post photos and videos to Facebook, your website, Twitter, Flickr, or an FTP site to show those that aren't there what they are missing.

196. Build attendance by creating a STAR program for first-time attendees.
Allow new attendees to enjoy a VIP experience. Offer them preferred seating at the general sessions and luncheons and acknowledge them publicly. Give them the opportunity to network with the board. Have an orientation program.

197. Utilize the relationships that your sponsors and exhibitors have with their clients and prospects.
Encourage sponsors and exhibitors to bring their top accounts to the meeting. Provide free or reduced-rate expo hall or full meeting registrations if they use the sponsor's code when registering.

198. Expand outside the association world.
Consider expanding outside your normal circles of influence. Invite corporate executives to join the association executive sphere. Communicate the relevance of your events to those on leadership/management tracks by offering CEO-level round tables, opportunities to network with other industry leaders, etc.

199. Utilize flip cameras.
Give flip cameras to a group of attendees with specific interview questions. Have them interview other attendees about the meeting. The peer-to-peer interaction engages attendees, and the video clips can be used for numerous promotional opportunities.

7 Digital Ideas to "Socialize" Your Next Tradeshow

Here are seven inexpensive but effective tradeshow marketing tactics for the digital age, tactics you can begin using today to build awareness and, most importantly, attendance for your next big event.

1. Use Smart, Focused Email Marketing

Most associations send one major communication per month to generate awareness about an event, which is fine. But once a potential attendee is in the communications stream, the goal should be to convert that person to an attendee by hitting them with progressively focused messages at the right time and in the most personal way possible.

2. Go Wild with Social Media

- Use social media listening tools to learn what people are saying and where they are saying it, then tailor your show's programming accordingly.
- Use Google docs to assign tasks and meetings and to make the calendar and information sharing more collaborative.
- Short on budget? Use EventBrite or another shareable, transactional registration system.
- Create a Facebook event—promote the event.
- Create a Facebook group—promote the group.
- Create a LinkedIn group—promote the group.
- Create a YouTube channel—promote the channel (see the trend here?).
- Create an open blog for the conference. Tap association employees, exhibitors, and key members to lead the conversation, and promote the blog. Enable this blog for mobile phones.
- Shamelessly promote and post social media communication leading up to, at, and after the event (Twitter).
- Call out your URL in everything you do.

3. Incorporate Video in Your Online Approach

Video continues to be the best way to engage the casual web user, so if you have any video whatsoever that's relevant to your show's topics, develop a branded YouTube channel (it's free!) to house this material. Then, use the embed code (also free) to incorporate those videos into your website and other communications. Also, buy a Flip camera to document the show. (For more on making your own videos and creating a channel online, read "Create a YouTube Channel for Your Association" by Renato Cruz Sogueco from the August 2009 issue of *TechnoScope.)*

4. Make Your Content Sharable

Forget about forward-to-a-friend functionality. Instead, try standardizing shareability of all website content on social networks through tools like Share This or Add This. Everything should be shareable.

5. Measure Better to Manage Better

To improve content maintenance, achieve better data integration, and enable measurement online and off, associations should invest in a contact or content management platform like Conversen or Eloqua (there are dozens on the market). If you're relying on an antiquated legacy system, you're just not getting the insights that inform smarter strategy.

6. Grab the Low-Hanging Search Engine Fruit

When considering *paid search* options, buy keywords by industry, issue, speaker, topic, and test performance. Then optimize on the fly. You're only paying for clicks. For *unpaid search*, there are a number of ways to improve organic search performance:

- Look at member surveys, particularly open-ended answers, to inform keyword strategy.
- Optimize each webpage with title tags, image tags, and metatags.
- Launch a link-building effort to enhance organic optimization.
- The more videos and shareable content on your site, the better you'll perform on Google.

7. Jazz Up Your Press Release

Traditional press releases are boring. Consider an interactive news release template that includes shareable photos and videos and provides easy ways to connect with traditional media as well as bloggers and trade journalists. Content can be repurposed from existing assets.

When it comes to thinking digital to boost awareness and attendance for your next tradeshow, it doesn't really matter *where* you start as long as you start. The need to use every tool in the shed has never been greater.

Excerpted from: Quigley, Shaun. "7 Digital Ideas to 'Socialize' Your Next Tradeshow." *Meetings & Expositions,* May 2010.

CONTINUE TO GENERATE CREATIVE IDEAS ON YOUR OWN

No matter how many ideas you can take from your colleagues, sometimes you will need to generate some internally. Most resources on idea generation and implementation process suggest three sequential stages: (1) use creative thinking to imagine the possibilities, (2) use critical thinking to evaluate the options, and (3) use constructive thinking to plan your implementation. Here's how you can put these three types of thinking to use toward the goals of building meeting attendance, enhancing member engagement and excitement about your meetings, and generating revenue.

Stage One—Creative Thinking: What?

The goal of the creative thinking process is to answer the "what" question, generating the maximum number of possibilities for the area you are looking to innovate: *What* could we do? *Quantity* is the definition of success for this step. Identifying more possibilities often is achieved by: (1) initially setting a numerical goal for the total number of ideas sought; "Let's generate 100 ideas for enhancing the exhibitor experience" and (2) listening for the content behind a specific idea and then inviting more possibilities for that concept: "Changing the registration layout area is a great example of making the meeting environment more welcoming. What are other ways we could do that?"

Stage Two—Critical Thinking: Which?
The goal of the critical thinking step is to evaluate all of the creative possibilities just generated and to determine which ideas you might want to move forward. *Quality* is the definition of success for this step. To make quality choices, first establish a few key factors everyone can use to evaluate each idea. Applying shared criteria helps minimize selecting ideas just because a particular individual champions them or because they may be more politically popular. After you've compiled and averaged individuals' assessments, you can then engage everyone in a discussion of the top-ranked ideas and finalize your selections.

Stage Three—Constructive Thinking: How?
This stage takes the ideas selected during the evaluation process and completes the action planning for their successful implementation. This is the detail-oriented, analytical work that converts your macro-level ideas into micro-level tactics. Adopting a backwards planning approach during this stage is often beneficial: Imagine the chosen idea has just been completed. What occurred last? Now what had to happen just prior for that final step to occur? Continue to repeat this process working your way back to the adoption of the idea. Others find creating a "mindmap" can help with implementation, first noting the major areas of activity that will be required and then drilling down to the specific tactics for each of those areas.

If you want to increase the odds of generating and successfully implementing great ideas, you must execute these three types of thinking in the order presented. When working with others to do so, it often requires facilitation that keeps participants appropriately focused and evokes a willingness of those involved to suspend their natural thinking strength until the appropriate time in the process.

Many individuals and groups are better at critical and constructive thinking. They find themselves more challenged by generating an expansive and inventive list of possible ideas during the creative thinking stage. A few simple strategies for boosting your creative thinking capacity include:

- Increase the variety of the people with whom you interact, the places you visit, and the media you consume. Our regular routines can easily become ruts. By intentionally hanging out with different people in different places, and examining different media, you can refresh the thinking you bring to your work.
- Intentionally include some wild ideas. Without them you lack any really interesting possibilities upon which to build the idea-generation process.
- Ask a completely different question. Posing the same question you've explored repeatedly is unlikely to elicit new ideas and fresh thinking. Ask an intentionally different and provocative question and you'll likely get different and provocative thinking in return.
- Use a creative thinking process that honors both introverted and extroverted individuals. The typical brainstorming process begins by inviting people to "shout out" their ideas, something only appealing to extroverts. Include time for people to reflect on the question/creative need and to note their ideas in writing before voicing them in the group.

Jeffrey Cufaude is an architect of ideas, helping advance the association community through his writing, speaking (retreats, workshops, keynotes), and facilitating (strategic planning and innovation think tanks). Learn more at www.ideaarchitects.org or follow him at twitter.com/jcufaude.

SHARE TIPS WITH COLLEAGUES

In our ongoing effort to connect great ideas and great people, we're collecting tips and ideas on a variety of topics that will be reviewed, and ***if selected,*** will be published in a future publication—a collection of "199" tips on a particular topic. You can choose to be credited as a contributor and if your tip is published be listed in the book as such, or you can choose to remain anonymous. Either way, it's a chance to give back to your profession and help others achieve greater success.

If you have questions about our "199 Ideas" series, please contact the director of book publishing at books@asaecenter.org.

Following is the submission form. We prefer that you visit **www.asaecenter.org/sharemytip** to submit your tip electronically via our website. However, if you prefer, you may copy and submit the form by mail or fax to:

Attn: Director of Book Publishing
ASAE: The Center for Association Leadership
1575 I Street, NW
Washington, DC 20005-1103
Fax: (202) 220-6439

Share My Tip Form

Please select the appropriate category or categories for your tip submission:

Board & Volunteers

- ☐ Board Relations
- ☐ Volunteer Relations
- ☐ Volunteer Recruitment
- ☐ Volunteer Engagement
- ☐ Volunteer Retention/Rewarding

Meetings

- ☐ Sponsorships
- ☐ Connecting Attendees
- ☐ Enhancing Learning Experiences
- ☐ Exhibits
- ☐ Generating Additional Revenue
- ☐ Other: ______________

Finance

- ☐ Budgeting
- ☐ Cutting Expenses
- ☐ Other: ______________

Benchmarking & Research

- ☐ Increasing Response Rate
- ☐ Other: ______________

Membership

- ☐ Recruitment/Retention
- ☐ Communications
- ☐ Engagement
- ☐ Program Benefits
- ☐ Dues Structures
- ☐ Globalization
- ☐ Research
- ☐ Other: ______________

Technology

- ☐ Other: ______________

Time-Saving Tips

- ☐ Other: ______________

Please submit your tip below. Please limit to 500 characters. If you require more than 500 characters, please submit via email directly to books@asaecenter.org with the subject "Tip".

____

____

____

____

____

____

____

____

____

____

____

continued on next page...

Share My Tip Form

continued from previous page

Name: ____________________

Organization: ____________________

____

Email: ____________________

Please indicate whether you would like to remain anonymous or be credited as a tip contributor if your tip is published:

☐ Anonymous

☐ Yes, please list me as a contributor.

By submitting your tip, you represent and warrant that you are the sole author and proprietor of all rights in the work, that the work is original, that the work has not been previously published, that the work does not infringe any personal or property rights of another, that the work does not contain anything libelous or otherwise illegal, and that you have the authority to enter into this agreement and grant of license. You also agree that the work contains no material from other works protected by copyright that have been used without the written consent of the copyright owner and that ASAE: The Center for Association Leadership is under no obligation to publish your tip submission.

You also grant ASAE: The Center for Association Leadership the following rights: (1) to publish the work in all print, digital, and other known or unknown formats; (2) to reprint, make derivative works of, and otherwise reproduce the work in all print, digital, and other known or unknown formats; and (3) to grant limited sub-licenses to others for the right to reprint, make derivative works of, and otherwise reproduce the work in all print, digital, and other known or unknown formats.

Signature ____________________

Thank you for submitting your tip!